In a Class of Our Own
Secrets to Student Success

A how-to book for students at
high school, college and university.

Bonus Section: Interview Tips

Susan Kingsbury

Canadian Cataloguing in Publication Data

Kingsbury, Susan
    In a class of our own: secrets to student success: a how-to book for students at high school, college and university

"Bonus section: interview tips"
ISBN 0-9685549-0-3

    1. Students—Handbooks, manuals, etc. 2. Study skills.
3. Success. I. Title.

LB2395.K55 1999   371.8   C99-900923-0

In a Class of Our Own: Secrets to Student Success

Published by:
    KNG Enterprises
    P.O. Box 71007
    L'Esplanade Laurier
    181 Bank Street
    Ottawa, Ontario, Canada
    K2P 2L9

Cover and layout design by:
Richard N. Strong, R.G.D., MGDC, Ottawa, Ontario

Consulting services on publication by:
Elaine Kenney, Communication Matters, Ottawa, Ontario.

Printed and bound in Canada by:
Transcontinental Printing Inc., Toronto, Ontario

DEDICATION

This book is dedicated to my family for their support
over the past 15 years while I attended university:
Danny, Mathew, Natalie, Judy, Ken, Matthew, and Andrew.

Sincere thanks and appreciation to my mentor, best friend, and
husband, Bob, for his continued encouragement, guidance,
and inspiration throughout my journey.

Happiness lies in the joy of achievement and the thrill of creative effort.

Franklin Roosevelt

TABLE OF CONTENTS

HOW THIS BOOK WILL HELP YOU

Your success is the goal of this book. You can excel as a student, including as a mature student, at high school, college, or university. The practical techniques in this book apply to all scenarios, because the skills are transferable. The good study habits needed in high school are also necessary for university. What's more, the skills required in an academic setting—planning and organizing your work, concentrating, researching, writing and editing, and meeting deadlines—are also in demand in the workplace. By applying the techniques in this book, you'll see all-round gains. You will excel as a student and, in turn, as a worker.

Begin by getting energized about learning the secrets of life. Experience the joy associated with the wonder of learning new things and meeting new people. Challenge yourself to be the best you can be. Above all, believe in yourself. Imagine where you would like to be in a year, or two years. Dare to dream, and dare to make your dreams come true.

Remember, success, for the most part, is perseverance. Devote yourself to your objectives and do whatever it takes to achieve them. Believe in yourself and don't give up.

Be aware of your potential. See past mistakes as learning experiences and determine where you can improve. Know that you can recover and begin again. Think of the present and the future and tap into the different choices available. Do not limit yourself. Celebrate successes—you deserve it. The power is within you to determine how your life will evolve.

This book will help you achieve your goals and guide you through many kinds of learning situations. It should be used along with advice from your parents, teachers, and guidance counsellors.

Students like you, at high school, college and university, helped create this book. They also include mature students, students who work full-time and have children.

They join me in wishing you success as you define your dreams and set out to make them come true. Best wishes from all of us.

Susan Kingsbury

ACKNOWLEDGEMENTS

Special thanks to the focus group who contributed to this book:

Christine Davies, Gloucester, Ontario

Joumana El-Ghossein, Gloucester, Ontario

Andrew Moonsammy, Nepean, Ontario

Samantha Moonsammy, Nepean, Ontario

Anne Morin, Nepean, Ontario

Vicki Morin, Nepean, Ontario

Jordan Saucier, Ottawa, Ontario

Daniel Smith, Nepean, Ontario

Suzanne Tannouri, Gloucester, Ontario

Line Toutain, Orleans, Ontario

Natalie Wasserlauf, Nepean, Ontario

Jeff Wood, Nepean, Ontario

Ability can take
you to the top, but
it takes character to
keep you there.

Anonymous

FOREWORD

As Secretary of the Treasury Board, I have had the pleasure of working with Susan Kingsbury since the mid-1990s. Throughout our association, she has impressed me with her on the job professionalism and with her determination to succeed as a part-time university student.

During her academic pursuits, Susan has motivated and guided other students by sharing the learning techniques and practices she developed while reaching her goals. This book gives students an opportunity to learn and use these techniques to help achieve their own academic objectives. In particular, Susan has identified the most important issues facing students at all levels, whether at high school, college or university, and including mature students—that is, how to get organized, how to study, how to stay motivated. These and other topics discussed in the book demonstrate her dedication to achieving excellence in studies while adopting a healthy and balanced lifestyle. The book also explains how the skills needed for academic excellence are identical to those that spell success in the workforce.

I am especially pleased to lend my support to this book in my official capacity representing the employer of Canada's Public Service. When more students succeed, our nation benefits from the higher caliber of individuals available for employment. In particular, I would encourage those who benefit from this book to consider a career in Canada's newly revitalized Public Service.

Susan's book is appealing for many reasons. First, the types of issues addressed are important for all students. Second, the information is presented in an interesting and easy to read fashion. Finally, the book is versatile with pages for 'personal notes' where students can jot down ideas and goals, making the book their own learning assistant. Susan also gives public presentations to share what she has learned and motivates others to do their best. This book is an excellent extension of this activity, since it provides an invaluable collection of tools to enable anyone to excel in their studies. Those who use this book wisely will have a better chance to achieve their academic goals and truly be "In a Class of Their Own."

V. Peter Harder, Secretary,
Treasury Board of Canada

If we did all the things
we are capable of doing,
we would literally
astonish ourselves.

Thomas Edison

DARE TO DREAM: MY PERSONAL STORY

I want to share with you my personal story and explain how this book is one outcome of a journey that began 15 years ago. My purpose in telling this story is to demonstrate that with simple techniques and determination, you too can achieve your dreams. I hope that my experience motivates you to excel as a student and teaches you to believe in yourself.

A decade and a half ago I dared to dream. As a single parent with two young children and a high school education, I started university as a part-time mature student. I had plateaued in my job, and future prospects seemed dim. I dreamed of a better life for me and my children; it was up to me to make it come true. The key to this dream was education. I believed that I was up to the challenge.

Making the decision to begin university was an agonizing exercise in soul-searching. After all, I already had a full-time job, was a volunteer at a local dance studio, and was raising two young boys. The idea of adding more responsibility and work to my already busy schedule was frightening. The decision didn't take place over night. On the contrary, it resulted from an evolution that was taking place in my life, and many factors contributed to the final decision to register.

One early morning in August 1984, my sons and I headed out, and I registered at Carleton University in Ottawa, Canada, for my first credit course. To ensure that the boys behaved, I promised them breakfast afterward at McDonald's. My sons were part of my journey right from the beginning. As I completed the final paperwork for registration, I was so excited and proud of myself that I wanted to shout with joy. Little did I know that I was about to embark on one of the most important journeys of my life. Although I was happy, my stomach was also a little upset. Yes, I still had some reservations, but I tried to focus on my dream of a better life. So off we went and had breakfast. It was a perfect start to an important day.

My first class was a surprise for me. I felt a bit sorry for myself, because I was a single parent struggling to get ahead. But interestingly, many of the students in my class were in similar situations, and my mood quickly changed. Furthermore, I realized that students, young and older, shared many of the same kinds of challenges: balancing home, work, and studies; learning new skills; dealing with professors. In other words, most students were feeling the same pressures as I was. I was also fortunate to have a good professor and teaching assistant. One of the first things I did was meet with them and explain my situation. This proved to be a good strategy throughout my student years, particularly if I had work or family emergencies.

Although I received a high mark on my first essay for this first course, I failed the Christmas exam. I was ready to quit. But a friend persuaded me that with a little more effort, I could easily recover and still pass the course. Not being one who gives up easily, I found ways to do more within the limited time I had available for my studies. In the spring I passed with a B grade. I was thrilled. My mark motivated me to continue, and I haven't stopped since.

As I continued with my courses, I started to document the things I learned that helped me succeed. Later I started to give presentations to individuals and groups on how students can excel in their studies, remain motivated, and simplify their life. As I prepared hand-outs for these sessions, the idea came to me that perhaps these training aids should become a book. It was a long while before I began to take this idea seriously, however.

As my sons grew I taught them the same techniques I was using at university: how to study, get high marks, and organize their responsibilities. I realized that the same techniques I was using at university were also required at the high school level. It also became obvious that the same techniques and skills were necessary and valuable in the workforce or when doing volunteer work. If someone wanted to excel as a student or in other areas of life, my techniques could help them. At this point, the idea of producing a book became much stronger.

Education is much more than just learning what is in a text book. It can change your life in ways you never imagined and bring about many positive surprises. Let me share some of the things that happened to me to demonstrate that this book is based on my personal experience.

The key to success for students is to ensure that you integrate studying with the rest of your life. Especially if you have children, this is an opportunity to enhance your time with them, not reduce it. For example, when my boys were around 8 and 10 we started to do homework together at the kitchen table. This was time to share stories about our teachers and our courses. The boys learned first-hand that I had many of the same problems and concerns they did. They also learned how much I loved to learn and how to find interest in even the dullest of courses. Given that we had many of the same triumphs and challenges, the boys quickly began to have greater respect for me. They saw that I was working hard but was still able to give them time. Our journey was a team effort. We would work together and later enjoy a snack. I was right there to help if they had questions about their homework. This meant that homework became quality family time; this was one of the best surprises for me during my journey.

My sons also accompanied me to the university campus from time to time. When using the library, I brought food and toys to help occupy the boys. Generally, I would plan to be there for about two hours, with a number of short breaks so the boys could run outside and play. It was also an opportunity to show them the university setting. They were fascinated with the library, amazed that such a place existed with so many books, and people could actually check them out and read them. They were impressed with the 'artwork' on the walls of the tunnels that connect the various parts of the Carleton University campus, thinking it was really cool that adults painted stuff on walls. They found the cafeteria huge and the vending machines irresistible. (I always had change available for instant bribes.) Research at the library became a family outing and one that my sons remember to this day.

Mature students often worry about how studying will affect their spousal/ partner relationship. I too was concerned given that I had remarried. Yet if approached correctly, education can also improve that part of life. For example, one summer my husband decided that while I was taking a course he would do some volunteer work on the same evening. After my class and his volunteer work were over, we would meet for coffee and dessert. This was wonderful quality time together. We had something interesting and new to share, and we were both doing something productive. I was enhancing my career while he was contributing to the community. Both of us and the community were winners.

My sons benefited too. For high school students the challenge is how to organize studies while planning for extracurricular activities. I guided my sons through high school by showing them how to use a 'planner' and how to develop a homework and study schedule. They learned how to juggle priorities and make decisions, such as asking for a reduction in hours in their part-time jobs. These were the same kinds of decisions I was facing. In other words, we were sharing useful techniques to enhance all our lives. As well, I was able to tutor one of my sons who was going on to university. I had studied many of the themes and theories that he was learning in high school, so I could give him additional information and clarify difficult points. We spent hours this way—he in his room and I in mine, both working at our computers, shouting information back and forth to each other. When he was at university there was an extra bonus—imagine having your son pick up and return your library books! My good life had finally arrived.

To be successful—whether you are a high school, college, university, or mature student—it is important to include family members on your journey. For example, a cherished memory for me is the day I received my honours BA degree. Present at the ceremony were my husband, my two sons, my step daughter, her husband, and her two sons. I made sure that they were part of my dream early on. In fact, when my step-grandsons were very young, I showed them my psychology book. In it was a picture of a tongue, showing which parts sensed sweet and which sour. We would look at this picture before we had an ice cream cone, then test the accuracy of the picture with the sweet treat. Looking at that picture became a before-ice cream routine—and an easy way to teach them that learning is fun.

During the past 15 years I have been fortunate: interesting courses, good professors, and progressive managers at work who supported my academic objectives. Most important, I was blessed with a family that supported me through my education, especially my husband who also spent many hours in the library with me. In June 1998, I completed my MA and decided to focus on my part-time business as a public speaker—and to publish this book! One thing I learned is that studying is a part of my life, and I am not yet ready to give up the journey. In September 1998, I began another Masters program in Mass Communication at Carleton University, and I am thoroughly enjoying this new area of study.

During my journey, many changes have taken place. There have been births and deaths in the family, and I have remarried. There were many times when I cried, was exhausted, and questioned my choices. Yet during it all, I could see my new life emerging. I continued to believe in myself and my dream. I dared to dream, and it came true. Now I challenge you, whether at high school, college, or university, to dream your dream and change your life for the better.

15 SECRETS TO SUCCESS

1. See learning as an adventure.

2. Stay motivated and think positive.

3. Plan celebrations and include family and friends.

4. Reward yourself for achievements large and small.

5. Set personal goals for the school year.

6. Establish a quiet homework and study area and assemble the necessary tools.

7. Organize your efforts with a homework and study schedule.

8. Do important things first and focus on one thing at a time.

9. Overlearn, use flash cards, and audio tapes.

10. Get help early and always ask questions.

11. Build good peer and teacher relationships.

12. Manage your time and stress levels.

13. Be patient and persevere.

14. Get enough sleep, eat well, and exercise regularly.

15. Be proud of your accomplishments and believe in yourself.

Success is a journey, not a destination.

Anonymous

Preparing for the New School Year

➥ To be successful at school it is important to have the right tools. What you need depends on the courses that you take.

▶ See the new year as an adventure; you are in control of your destiny, so make it worthwhile.

▶ Imagine the good times you will have, the interesting things you will learn, and the new people you will meet.

▶ Be optimistic, recognizing up-front that your year will be both fun and hard work.

▶ Define your main goals for the year, for example—higher marks, better essays.

▶ Promise yourself that you will be the best you can be.

▶ Stay focused, persevere, and have a great year!

SUGGESTED TOOLS:

- ☐ study and homework area
- ☐ good chair
- ☐ foot rest
- ☐ reliable watch
- ☐ dictionary
- ☐ thesaurus
- ☐ verb book
- ☐ calculator
- ☐ stapler & staples
- ☐ 3 hole punch
- ☐ correction fluid
- ☐ glue stick
- ☐ scotch tape
- ☐ tape dispenser
- ☐ markers
- ☐ ruler
- ☐ scissors, paper clips
- ☐ pencils, pens
- ☐ eraser
- ☐ index cards
- ☐ index card holder

- ☐ planner/scheduler
- ☐ 3 ring binder, paper
- ☐ binders
- ☐ note books
- ☐ file folders
- ☐ blank tabs
- ☐ self-sticking notes/flags
- ☐ tape recorder
- ☐ batteries for recorder
- ☐ bookcase
- ☐ filing cabinet
- ☐ computer and supplies

OTHER:

- ☐ prepare coats
- ☐ prepare shoes/boots/gloves
- ☐ umbrella
- ☐ school bag
- ☐ lunch bag
- ☐ bus pass/tickets
- ☐ parking pass
- ☐ best route to school

You were born to win, but in order to become a winner you must plan to win and prepare to win. Then you can legitimately expect to win.

Anonymous

PERSONAL NOTES

What courses will you be taking?

_____

_____

_____

_____

What tools do you need and what do they cost?

_____

_____

_____

_____

Where and when will you buy the tools?

_____

_____

_____

_____

_____

_____

What books do you require?

What reward will you give yourself when everything is prepared for the school year?

Other comments

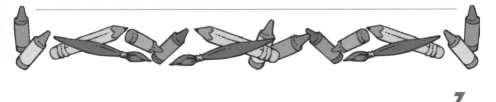

Maintaining Your Motivation

▱ Motivation is achieved primarily through a positive outlook and hard work. It is a commitment to yourself.

▶ Listen to positive and motivational messages, and surround yourself with upbeat people.

▶ Be inspired by other successful people and discover their secrets to achieving goals.

▶ Set realistic goals—things you can achieve, like raising your mark from a C to a C+ or B, not necessarily from a C to an A.

▶ Reward yourself after small achievements, such as finishing a reading assignment on time or doing well on a test.

▶ Relish your victories and learn from your mistakes.

▶ Believe in yourself. Never give up—persevere and be patient. Success does not happen overnight.

▶ Include your friends and family in your successes. They are important to your accomplishments, since they are part of your 'support system'.

► Get energized on life! Challenge and discard negative attitudes that bring you down or interfere with your goals.

► Imagine that you are an actor and pretend you are positive and enthusiastic. Surprisingly, you will find your mood may actually change for the better.

► Feeling down? Talk with someone who can help you. Don't let this feeling take control of you. If you can't get rid of the feeling, put a time limit on it. For example, submit to the 'blues' for two hours, then demand that positive attitudes return. Regain control of your feelings and usual good humour.

► If your down mood continues, discuss it with a parent, doctor, teacher, guidance counsellor or other adult you trust. You don't want the feeling to get worse, so it's important to seek help early.

► Remember, the key to being motivated is having a positive outlook. This is more than an attitude, *it's a way of life*.

If you hear a voice
within you say
'you cannot
paint,' then by
all means paint,
and that voice
will be silenced.

Vincent Van Gogh

PERSONAL NOTES

Who are some successful people and why do they inspire you?

_____

_____

_____

_____

How will you motivate yourself during the year?

_____

_____

_____

_____

What realistic goals do you have for the year?

_____

_____

_____

_____

_____

How are you going to involve your family and friends?

_____

_____

_____

_____

How are you going to handle your down moods?

_____

_____

_____

How will you reward yourself for your achievements?

_____

_____

_____

_____

Other comments.

_____

_____

_____

_____

Studying Successfully

✏️ Ensure that you have a designated area for homework and studying where you will not be interrupted.

▶ Overlearn your notes; this will raise your self-confidence.

▶ Make flash cards with main study points, and put the points on audio tapes to listen to.

▶ Integrate your studying by using the tapes and flash cards while on the bus, waiting in a line, or exercising on a stationary bike.

▶ To prepare for exams, have someone ask you questions or list questions that you can ask yourself later as a pre-test.

▶ Obtain a copy of previous exams if possible (university students will usually find exams at the Library).

▶ Develop a realistic study schedule. (Refer to the example in the 'positive thinking' section.) The more realistic your schedule is, the more likely you will follow it.

► Show your schedule to friends and family so that they know when not to disturb you.

► Ensure that you have everything you need to study: reading materials, notes, additional blank paper, pens, etc.

► Learn to say 'no' to other obligations during your exam period.

► Try to avoid cramming, as you will not retain much of what you studied after the exam. The trick is to understand as much information as possible at the beginning, so that when you review it, you will retain it more easily.

► Create a learning opportunity during short intervals when you have to fill in time—waiting on hold on the telephone, standing in line to get tickets, or during television commercials (use the mute button on the remote control!). Even if you have just 5 minutes, you should be able to learn a couple of points. When you first try this, it will seem that you are not absorbing anything. But once your brain has been trained to learn in a short period, this will be an effective studying technique.

I haven't failed,
I've found
10,000 ways
that don't work.

Thomas Edison

PERSONAL NOTES

What subjects will you put on flash cards and/or audio tapes?

_____

_____

_____

_____

Where will you study?

_____

_____

_____

What tools do you need to study?

_____

_____

_____

When and where will you get previous exams?

_____

_____

What other activities take place during exam time?

How will you balance these activities with studying?

What rewards will you give yourself for accomplishing study goals?

Other comments.

Taking Notes

Would you like notes that are easy to read and that will help you study better? Then you may want to consider the 'bullet method'. The bullet method and the traditional method are compared below:

Traditional Method:

Subject: Winterlude

Winterlude takes place in Ottawa annually in February. This festival is one of Ottawa's biggest tourist attractions. Activities take place across the National Capital Region and particularly at the canal, which is known as the longest skating rink in the world.

Bullet Method:

Winterlude
- Ottawa every February
- one of the biggest tourist attractions
- activities in NCR and along canal
- Ottawa has longest skating rink in the world

Benefits of the Bullet Method:

1. Saves time and energy because you only write down the most important ideas.

2. Notes are clearer and easier to read.

3. This method helps facilitate studying. For example:
   - first memorize your pages then place a card on the right-hand side of your paper to cover the bullet details so that only the headings on the left side are showing,
   - recite out loud the bullets associated with each heading
   - remove the card to check what you have said
   - put the main headings on flash cards (carry them with you and review at the bus stop, while eating lunch, standing in line at the movie theatre, cash machine, or grocery store
   - headings can be recorded on tape (listen to it while you are mowing the lawn, doing the dishes, going for a walk)

When taking notes:

▶ Write the course title, teacher's name, date and page number on all your notes.

▶ Read notes after each class so that the ideas stay with you; highlight main points.

▶ File chronologically at home for future reference. As a rule, don't lend your notes; you may have trouble getting them back or they may come back in poor shape or out of order.

It is not because
things are difficult
that we do not dare,
it is because we do
not dare that they
are difficult.

Seneca

20

PERSONAL NOTES

Learning to Focus and Listen

 Staying focused and listening effectively are abilities that have to be developed. Few people are born with these skills for success. These abilities are interrelated and interdependent.

FOCUSING ENABLES YOU TO:	LISTENING EFFECTIVELY ALLOWS YOU TO:
- work more efficiently, as it saves time	- absorb more details
- get it right the first time	- understand or to ask questions the first time around
- do a better job on one thing at a time	- show a caring side when you are listening to someone
- conserve your energy	- develop other skills, e.g., consultation, negotiation, group dynamics, etc.

▶ To remain focused, it is best to work where you are not disturbed; be organized and stay alert.

▶ Eat properly—if you are hungry or thirsty you will not remain focused.

- ▶ Get enough sleep. Sleep deprivation reduces alertness and affects your ability to concentrate and remember.

- ▶ Ensure that your notes and books are organized. Chaos drags on your subconscious, undermining focus and attentiveness.

- ▶ To strengthen your listening skills, tape a favourite song or news broadcast for one or two minutes as you listen to it. Then write down the details. Now play the tape and see how many details you remembered. Continue this practice to develop your listening skills. Increase the listening time as you improve.

- ▶ To develop concentration and memory skills, have someone place objects on a tray and show them to you for 30 seconds. After the tray is removed, list its contents, then compare what you listed with what is on the tray. Vary this exercise with different amounts of time and the number of objects on the tray.

- ▶ Listening skills are particularly important to complement other home, school, and work skills. They can contribute to your success with people and give you a competitive edge. That's why it's important to cultivate this skill early.

In the middle
of difficulty
lies opportunity.

Albert Einstein

PERSONAL NOTES

How can you be more organized?

_____

_____

_____

_____

What nutritious foods should you eat?

_____

_____

_____

_____

What foods should you avoid?

_____

_____

_____

_____

_____

_____

When do you need sleep most; how many hours a night are right for you?

_____

_____

_____

_____

_____

How can you organize your notes and books?

_____

_____

_____

_____

How can you strengthen your listening skills?

_____

_____

_____

_____

How can you strengthen your concentration skills?

_____

_____

_____

_____

How will you reward yourself for strengthening your skills?

_____

_____

_____

_____

Other comments.

_____

_____

_____

_____

_____

_____

_____

Achieving Good Exam Marks

✎ Cultivate good study habits.

▸ Develop a study schedule for exams and stick to it.

▸ Make sure you have no extracurricular activities or work during exam week.

▸ Check out where you will be writing the exams, to familiarize yourself with the room and setting before exam day. This way you will be more comfortable with your exam environment.

▸ Get help or tutoring early if you need it.

▸ Keep on top of your work.

▸ Meet essay and assignment deadlines.

▸ Ask for guidance from your teacher. Here are some questions to ask:

1. What should I focus on, or what is absolutely important? For example, should I study:
   - what is in the book, or what we learned in class?
   - what we learned for the full year, or just the second half?

2. Are there certain sections or themes that will not be on the exam?

3. What types of questions will be on the exam, e.g., fill-in-the-blanks, multiple choice, true or false, quotations, definitions, or short or long essay questions?

4. Will questions be weighted and, if so, how? Will fill-in-the-blank questions get more marks than the short essay questions?

5. How long will the exam be?

6. Will the exam be hand-written or will we be using a computer?

► Tips on answering an essay question on an exam:
    - write an introduction, a body, and a conclusion
    - give the pros and cons of the argument and cite sources
    - provide some statistics and quotations
    - tell an interesting story
    - analyze the data and provide your opinion

► Think positive, believe in yourself, and know that with hard work you can achieve your goals.

► Plan to reward yourself for your future good mark on the exam.

Before every-
thing else,
getting ready
is the secret of
success.

Henry Ford

PERSONAL NOTES

Do you need help? If so, whom should you see and when?

_____

_____

_____

_____

_____

_____

_____

_____

What are the various things you need to do to be ready to write the exam? What is the deadline for each thing?

_____

_____

_____

_____

_____

_____

What reward will you give yourself once you have finished your exam?

_____

_____

_____

_____

_____

How will you include your family and friends in your accomplishments? Is there anyone you should thank?

_____

_____

_____

_____

_____

Other comments.

_____

_____

_____

_____

Preparing for Exam Day

- Ensure that you get a full 8 hours sleep or more the night before.

- Eat nutritiously the day of your exam. For example, if your exam is at 9 a.m. eat a good breakfast, so that your energy stays high for the morning.

- Depending on when your exam is scheduled, plan an hour for review before the start time.

- Get to your exam room 15 to 30 minutes before starting time.

- Ensure that your schedule is clear the day of the exam and the day before, so you can focus only on the exam.

- Do not take unnecessary phone calls, e-mails, or other interruptions on exam day or the day before. Deal only with important things. If something does not require your immediate attention, wait until after the exam.

- During the exam, make sure you understand each question you are answering.

- Review all the questions on the exam first. Always answer the questions you can answer well before moving on to the others. Let your subconscious work on the other questions while you answer the ones you know.

- Do an outline of the essay questions before writing them.

- Calculate how much time you need for the various sections of the exam so that you have ample time to finish it.

- If you are writing an essay question, double space it.

- If you are sitting beside someone whose behaviour—chewing gum, coughing, fidgeting—is disturbing you, ask the teacher to move you so you can concentrate.

- Dress comfortably for the exam.

- Think positively and believe that you will do well.

- Plan for a celebration with family or friends once the exam is finished. Reward yourself.

The future belongs
to those who believe

---

in the beauty of
their dreams.

Eleanor Roosevelt

EXAM CHECKLIST

What is your personal goal regarding this exam?

_____

What are the details of the exam?

date: _____

time: _____

place: _____

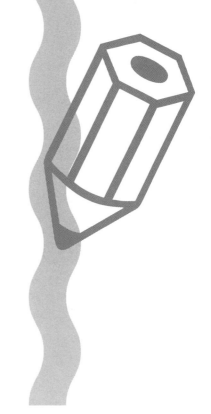

What are some things that you may want to bring with you?

- Pens, Pencils

- Eraser

- Ruler

- Calculator/Batteries

- Diskette

- Correction Fluid

- Notes/Flash Cards

- Text Books/Dictionary

- Water/Juice

- Tissue

- Glasses

- Lozenges/Candy/Gum

- Medication

- Watch

- Bus Pass/Tickets or Parking Pass

- Other

_____

_____

_____

_____

_____

_____

_____

_____

_____

_____

PERSONAL NOTES

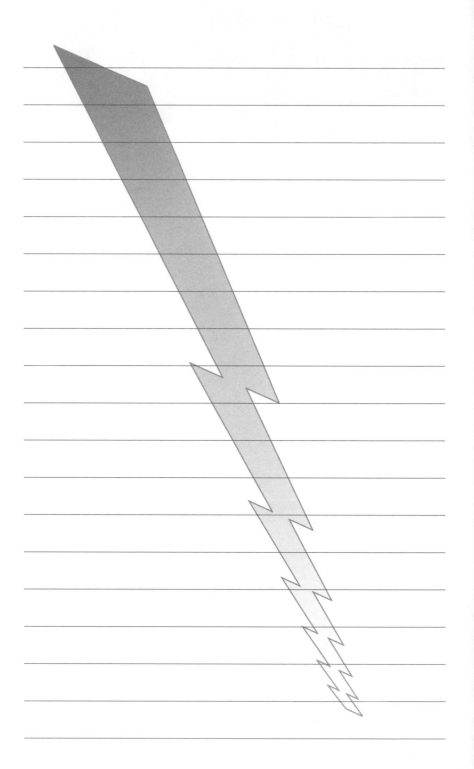

Raising Low Grades

✎ Always ask for help as soon as you suspect that you need it.

▶ Ask 'A' students how they get their high marks.

▶ Make a homework and study schedule and stick to it.

▶ Consider doing homework or studying with a partner or group to improve your marks. For some students this is a good method.

▶ If you are working part-time or doing volunteer work, reduce the hours devoted to these activities until your marks improve.

▶ Ask yourself some fundamental questions:

What are my strengths and my weaknesses?

Are my notes orderly and easy to read?

Am I capturing the main points of class lectures?

Do I understand what I'm learning?

Am I distracted in class (home, work or school problems?)

Do I like this subject? If not, how can I get interested in it?

Am I missing too many classes?

Am I putting in enough time on my homework and studying?

Am I motivated? If not, why?

Do I have a health problem that is interfering with my progress?

Am I sleepy or not eating properly?

Have I sought school counselling or discussed how I can improve my marks with a friend or family member?

▸ Once you know what the problem is, commit yourself to making the necessary changes to improve your marks.

▸ Remember, there are always ways to recover from low marks, even if it's late in the year.

Destiny is not a matter of chance, it is a matter of choice.

Anonymous

Whom can you ask for help?

_____

_____

_____

_____

Who are the 'A' students you know?

_____

_____

_____

_____

Do you study better on your own or with a partner or group?

_____

_____

Who might be your study partner or a member of your study group?

_____

_____

_____

How can you and when should you reduce your work hours to concentrate on your studies?

_____

_____

_____

What other improvements do you need to make to raise your marks?

_____

_____

_____

_____

_____

_____

What rewards will you give yourself as you plan to improve your marks and achieve your goals?

_____

_____

_____

_____

ABcABcABcABc

How will you thank the people who helped you?

_____

_____

_____

_____

_____

Other comments.

_____

_____

_____

_____

_____

_____

_____

_____

Building Winning Relationships with Teachers

Having good relationships with teachers is essential for succeeding in school. How can you enlist their help to achieve your goals?

▶ Meet deadlines for essays and assignments.

▶ Provide credible reasons if deadlines cannot be met.

▶ Ask for their guidance on how to do assignments.

▶ Leave your desk tidy and place garbage in proper containers.

▶ Let them know when you have enjoyed a particular lecture, reading, or outing, and explain why.

▶ If you don't understand what the teacher has said, ask for a further explanation right away—if you are confused, others may be as well (there is no such thing as a stupid question).

▶ Never be rude or talk back—state your case calmly and rationally.

▶ Smile and use positive body language and words.

- ▶ If you are not feeling well, let the teacher know before class.

- ▶ Ask your parents to call the teachers a couple of times during the year to ensure that you are doing o.k. (this is over and above the regular parent-teacher interviews).

- ▶ Ask your teachers if you can help them, for example, clean the boards, turn on the computers etc.

- ▶ If you're having difficulty with a particular teacher, try to find his or her good points, and look for a subject or interest you both have in common, for example, movies, camping, etc.

- ▶ Thank teachers for the positive things they do.

- ▶ Enjoy your time in class; remember that you are learning new things that make you an interesting person.

Many receive
advice, only
the wise profit
from it.

Syrus

PERSONAL NOTES

What can you do to strengthen your relationships with teachers?

_____

_____

_____

_____

_____

What positive words should you use?

_____

_____

_____

_____

What positive actions will demonstrate your desire to establish a good relationship with a teacher?

_____

_____

_____

_____

_____

_____

_____

How might you thank your teachers for their help?

_____

_____

_____

_____

_____

_____

What fun or new things have you been learning or doing at school that make you a more interesting person?

_____

_____

_____

_____

_____

Other comments.

_____

_____

_____

_____

_____

_____

_____

_____

_____

_____

Starting Fresh in January

Opportunity knocks! The new year gives you another chance to evaluate your progress and make improvements. Essentially, it's back to basics.

▶ You still need the proper tools and work area to do your homework. Do you have everything you need? Do you need to make any adjustments?

▶ Review your homework and study schedule. Ensure that it still meets your needs and that you still follow it. (Refer also to the sections on achieving good exam marks, raising low grades, and studying successfully.)

▶ Don't get discouraged if your marks are low; you still have time to recover.

▶ If you need help with your studies, see your teachers early and get a tutor or a friend to help you if necessary.

▶ Take advantage of the spring break to study or do additional homework.

▶ Make a commitment to give it your best shot until the end of the school year.

- ▶ Reward yourself from time to time for meeting your objectives.

- ▶ Believe that you can improve your grades and meet your objectives.

- ▶ Finish school on a high note and look forward to a great summer.

The difference between ordinary and extraordinary is that little extra.

PERSONAL NOTES

What will you do to motivate yourself for the rest of the year?

_____

_____

_____

_____

What changes do you want to make to your homework and study schedules?

_____

_____

_____

_____

_____

How will you make these changes and when?

_____

_____

_____

_____

Other comments.

_____

_____

_____

_____

_____

_____

_____

_____

_____

Balancing School and a Part-time Job or Volunteer Work

✏️ Always remember that school is your first priority and a job/ voluntary work is secondary.

▶ The types of things that you take into consideration for a job also hold true for volunteer work as listed below.

▶ Choose a job that you like and that gives you some flexibility in the number of hours you work.

▶ Pick a job that is close to home or has a direct bus route to your home. Knowing how much travelling time is involved will help you judge whether the job is for you.

▶ If the job offers flexibility, the number of hours you choose to work will depend on your school demands and your need for money. Try not to commit yourself too heavily.

▶ Discuss your job choice with someone you trust—a parent or school guidance counsellor—to see whether it will balance well with home and school commitments.

▶ Try to reduce your job hours during exam time. If this is not possible, start studying for exams early to give yourself every opportunity for good marks.

▶ Learn the health and safety code of the place you work. Ensure that the equipment you are using is within health and safety standards. If not, ask for changes or stop working there.

▶ Have fun and enjoy the chance to learn new things.

We are continually
faced by great
opportunities
brilliantly disguised as
insoluble problems.

Anonymous

PERSONAL NOTES

What types of jobs interest you?

_____

_____

_____

_____

What organizations will you contact for work or volunteer opportunities? To whom should you speak?

_____

_____

_____

_____

_____

_____

How many hours can you devote to a job and when?

_____

_____

_____

Other comments.

JOB/VOLUNTEER WORK CHECKLIST
(Key Factors to Consider)

Name of employer _____

Location _____

Travel:
- how to get there
- number of hours to commute
- cost of commuting

Hours of work: _____

Salary (not applicable if volunteer work):

Type of work:
- labour
- office
- dealing with the public

Work arrangement:
- part-time
- full-time
- seasonal
- contract

Conditions of work:
a lot of:
- reading
- sitting
- standing
- lifting
- computer work
- driving
- busy (identify peak periods)
- slow
- high pressure
- overtime
- separate or shared office
- work with heavy or dangerous machinery
- work with chemicals

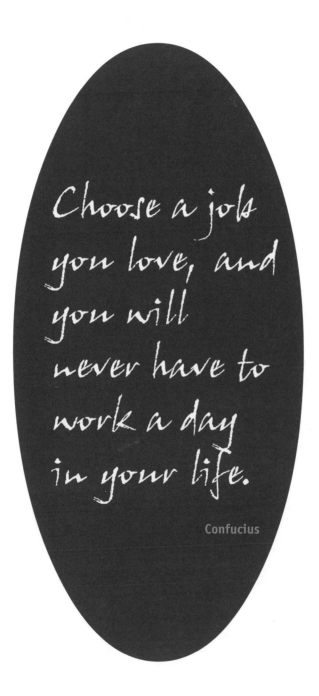

Choose a job you love, and you will never have to work a day in your life.

Confucius

Saving and Spending Effectively

Do you want to buy that new sweater, or are you saving toward your university tuition? In both cases, with a little effort and imagination you can reach your goal. Here are some helpful tips.

▶ Identify short- and long-term financial goals.

▶ Develop a budget and stick to it.

▶ Shop around to find a savings account that has the highest interest rate and meets your needs.

▶ Use a bank, trust company, or credit union that has the services you need; do not pay for services you are unlikely to use.

▶ Seek financial advice from an adviser at a financial institution.

▶ Do not write cheques on your savings account unless absolutely necessary.

▶ The first $50 to save is the hardest.

- Once you have a nest egg consider a Registered Retirement Savings Plan (RRSP) or other financial vehicle that offers a better rate of return.

- Before buying something, ask yourself if you really need it; what would the consequences be if you bought it / didn't buy it.

- Have fun with your money; save the amount called for in your budget, but also spend some money on yourself so that you will continue to be motivated to save.

- Use coupons, eat at restaurants, and go to movies that offer special discounts.

- Purchase things on sale. Look for clothes, books, etc. at second-hand shops.

- When possible, borrow instead of purchasing.

- Limit gifts to under $8—candles, fancy soaps, picture frames, paperback books.

- Budgeting is a skill that will serve you well throughout your life.

You cannot climb the ladder of success with your hands in your pockets.

Anonymous

PERSONAL NOTES

What things would you like to save for? What would be the consequences if you bought / didn't buy them?

Things	Consequences

What are your short-term financial goals?

_____

_____

_____

_____

What are your long-term financial goals?

_____

_____

_____

_____

What financial institutions will you call to see which has the best interest rate on savings accounts or guaranteed investment certificates? Who is the contact person?

_____

_____

_____

_____

What gifts do you plan to buy over the next year? How much will you spend?

_____

_____

_____

_____

How will you reward yourself after you have saved your first $50? $100? $500? $1,000?

_____

_____

_____

_____

_____

Other comments.

_____

_____

_____

_____

_____

Year End:
Congratulations Students!

Celebrate your successes!

▶ Include family and friends in celebrations you plan.

▶ Send thank you notes to people who helped you with your accomplishments.

▶ Review how you achieved your goals.

▶ Identify how you improved yourself over the past year.

▶ List the changes and improvements you want to make next year. File your list away so that you can refer to it in September or when you return to school.

▶ File all your school notes and examinations.

▶ Enjoy your summer— you deserve it.

To keep the body in good health is a duty . . . Otherwise we shall not be able to keep our mind strong and clear.

Buddha

PERSONAL NOTES

What celebrations have you planned with family and friends?

_____

_____

_____

_____

What special rewards do you have planned for yourself?

_____

_____

_____

_____

_____

What were your key successes this year? What contributed to these achievements?

_____

_____

_____

_____

What changes or improvements would you like to make for next year?

_____

_____

_____

_____

_____

_____

_____

What fun and interesting things did you learn this year?

_____

_____

_____

Other comments.

_____

_____

_____

Graduation Day

✏️ The most important thing you can do on graduation day is **attend**.

▶ This is your day to pat yourself on the back and be recognized for all your hard work and perseverance.

▶ Share this moment with those who are important to you.

▶ Make it a very special day. Decorate the house, have a get-together celebration with friends and family.

▶ Assign someone to take pictures when you receive your certificate or degree.

▶ This is your time to reflect on your accomplishments. Remember the fun, exciting, and interesting times. Remember also the hard times and how you overcame those challenges.

▶ Keep a journal of this special day so that you will always have it to read as you go through life. It's a keepsake that will remind you of the satisfaction and pride you felt when you achieved your goal, your dreams for the future as you thought about the next stage on your journey, and even your bittersweet thoughts about leaving one phase of life behind to move on to the next.

Whatever you can do or dream you can, begin it. Boldness has genius, power, and magic in it. Begin now.

Goethe

dreams

dreams

Positive Thinking

▱ Positive thinking is more than just thinking 'happy' thoughts. It's a way to bring out the best in you and give you a more balanced perspective on life. Positive thinking is about building a strong character. This page is linked to the one on 'motivation'.

▶ Positive thinking means setting goals, identifying the steps to reach each goal, describing what it will take to do the steps, and determining deadlines. It is a form of personal management. Through it all you need to believe in yourself, work hard toward your objectives, and remain relentlessly optimistic even during times of hardship. This is when your inner strength will be tested. Be patient and persevere.

▶ When people think positively, beneficial chemicals known as endorphins are released in the body. They contribute to your sense of well-being, so if you are in a good frame of mind, you are already helping your body help you. Exercise also releases endorphins. That is why it is important to participate in physical activity. Thinking negative thoughts produces negative reactions in your body, putting you at a disadvantage.

▶ Be smart. Think positive.

▶ Try to be optimistic at all times and relish the opportunity to live and learn.

▶ Focus on the good things in your life, no matter how small.

- Learn to use positive phrases in your writing and when you speak.

- Positive words to use (see also the list starting on page 82): celebrate, up-beat, find the solution, the lessons learned, contributing to the community, enjoy, like, pleased, willing, rejoice, relish, success, persevere, patience.

- Try to use a new positive word or phrase each day, so that you learn to incorporate them in your everyday speech.

- When negative thoughts enter your mind, don't let them stay; tell your subconscious to send them away or find a positive word or thought to replace it. You have the power to control what you think and do.

- Always try to find the meaning in things that are difficult or that go wrong; learn from them. If something goes wrong do not give up. Perseverance and patience are keys to success.

- Enjoy the ride. If a goal takes a long time to complete—what's your rush? Eventually you will get what you want if you hang in. Devote yourself to your objective and remain focused.

Example:

Goal: To get a higher mark on your December examination.

Try to start a good month before, so that if a conflict arises you will still be prepared.

Deadline: exam is on December 10th

Steps: 1. Get a calendar.
2. Develop a homework and study plan.
3. See teacher about examination.
4. Reduce work/volunteer hours two weeks before exam.
5. Tell parents or relevant persons when exam will take place.

How to accomplish steps:
1. Get a calendar to develop study plan and mark important dates (by Nov. 5).
2. Talk to employer about reducing hours (Nov. 5).
3. Talk to parents or others about planned family outings or events. e.g., birthdays, sports play-offs etc., that you need to be involved in during the target period (Nov. 5).
4. Make an appointment to see the teacher a good month before the exam (Nov. 7).
5. Make sure notes are up to date and easy to read (by Nov. 9).
6. Make study flash cards (Nov. 7-9).
7. Finalize study plan (Nov. 9).
8. Begin studying and follow study schedule (Nov. 10).

▶ Once you meet your goal, celebrate your success. If you did not meet your goal then see teacher and ask for guidance.

We are what we think. All that we are arises with our thoughts. With our thoughts, we make our world.

Buddha

Positive Words & Phrases

ACCOMPLISH

ACHIEVE

AMIABILITY

BLESSINGS

BRISK

CAPTIVATING

COMMITMENT

CONTENT

ENCHANTED

ENCOURAGE

ENJOYING

CELEBRATE

CHALLENGE

CHEERFUL

CHEERING

DEVOTION

CURIOUS

COURTEOUS

CONTRIBUTE

GIGGLE

GLEE

EXHILARATING

FASCINATING

FESTIVITY

GOOD TIMES

HEIGHTEN

HELPFUL

HONOUR

GLORIFY

GLISTENING

EXCEED

EXCEL

EXCELLENT

EXCEPTIONAL

FIND THE SOLUTION

FLOURISH

FORTUNE

HOPE

ILLUMINATIONS

LUCKY

IMAGINE

MAGIC

INSPIRE

INTERESTING

JOYFUL

JUBILANT

LAUGH

MERRYMAKING

MILK AND HONEY

OPPORTUNITY

PEACE OF MIND

OUTSTANDING

OPTIMISTIC

PERSEVERE

PLAYFULNESS

PLEASED

WELL-BEING

WILLING

SERENITY

SINCERE

PROGRESS

PROSPEROUS

RAINBOW

SMILES

SPARKLING

REWARD

RECOGNITION

REJOICE

POSITIVE

(PERSONALITY)
POLISHED

PLEASING LESSONS LEARNED

LIGHT-HEARTED

RESPECTFUL

REWARD

SEE THE
BRIGHT SIDE

STARS (SKY)

SUCCEED

SUNSHINE

SURPASS

TINSEL

THRIVING

UP-BEAT

WARM WELCOME

TWINKLE

TRIUMPH

TRANSCEND

PERSONAL NOTES

The talent of success is nothing more than doing what you can do well, and doing well whatever you do.

Henry Wadsworth Longfellow

Examples of Personal Rewards

⊯ Treating yourself to a special food or drink.

▸ Relax in a bath and light some scented candles.

▸ Energize yourself through music.

▸ Surprise someone special with a phone call.

▸ Feel alive with a good massage.

▸ Contact your inner self through meditation.

▸ Exercise: walk, jog, roller-blade, swim.

▸ Attend a movie, concert, or sports event.

▸ Invite friends for a party.

▸ Create through cooking.

▸ Buy something new.

▸ Eat at one of your favourite restaurants.

- ▶ Read a motivational book.

- ▶ Enjoy a family outing.

- ▶ Thank someone.

- ▶ Go to bed earlier or later.

- ▶ Rent a movie.

- ▶ Challenge yourself to a puzzle.

- ▶ Undertake a hobby.

- ▶ Volunteer for a community event.

You get the best out of others when you give the best of yourself.

Harvey Firestone

Examples of Family / Friend Celebrations

- Celebrate at a restaurant.

- Have a special cake at a family dinner.

- Enjoy a family outing—a picnic, sports event, movie, play mini golf.

- Send family members a card/letter of thanks.

- Visit family friends together.

- Do a specific 'big' chore for the family to show that you appreciate all the help they have given you and you want to reciprocate—for example, a family weekend opening up the cottage, cleaning the yard, painting the apartment.

- When you hold celebrations, make sure you thank everyone who helped you and share your successes with them.

- Celebrate after you have
    - just registered or begun a new year (like a kick-off)
    - received your first marks
    - finished writing all your exams
    - completed writing your essay
    - done your first presentation
    - finished your year

It is not enough to have a good mind; the main thing is to use it well.

Rene Descartes

Complementary Courses

Expand your mind and your options by taking other short-term courses. They will complement what you do at school as well as what you do at work. Most of these courses are inexpensive and usually only take a few hours to complete. But their payoff is big. They include courses on how to

- make presentations
- write an essay
- take notes and study
- speed read
- make flip charts
- use the library, including the National Archives
- use the Internet
- use a computer for word processing, graphics
- write a memorandum or letter
- do research
- deal with difficult people
- be assertive
- work in a team setting
- communicate
- apply makeup
- identify your colours (clothes)
- dress for success

Only those who
will risk going
too far can
possibly find
out how far
one can go.

T.S. Eliot

How School Links to World of Work and Volunteering

✏️ Some people believe that school does not teach us about the 'real' working world. This is a myth. School does teach us things that are fundamental to workplace success. Here are some of the school-learned abilities that can be transferred anywhere:

▶ At school you learn how to
  - keep notes and files and to do neat work
  - solve problems, follow instructions and meet deadlines
  - read, write, give presentations, and do projects
  - do research in a library
  - use a computer
  - support the school through extracurricular events
  - be punctual and follow a dress code
  - develop self-respect, confidence, and independence
  - strengthen interpersonal skills with parents, teachers, friends, others
  - share responsibilities and tasks with others; work individually or as a team

▶ All these competencies will also help you to do well on the job or as a volunteer. Many of them will also help you organize your personal life and interact with family and friends. This is why school is so important. After all, you want to be the best you can be so that you get the most out of life, and so that you will eventually be able to give back to the community and help others.

- ▶ The school setting is where you should try everything you can to make yourself the best you can be. Don't focus too much on what others are doing. Compete with yourself first and foremost.

- ▶ Success is 5% inspiration and 95% perspiration. Most people succeed because they remain relentlessly optimistic and they persevere.

- ▶ Genius is in the details—extreme genius is in the final details.

- ▶ Strive for excellence.

The mind is like
a parachute—it
doesn't work
unless it's open.

Anonymous

Balancing Work, Home, and Studies as a Mature Student

▱ In addition to the suggestions presented in the previous pages, the key to your success as a mature student is to integrate your studies with your work and family life.

▸ A common belief is that studying will take time away from your family. However, with organization and implementation of the suggestions in this book, your quality family time should improve. It is better to see your studies as an integral part of your life, so that you can involve your family and friends in your goals.

▸ Focus on one course at a time. Try not to think about the 'big picture'; you may become discouraged. Know in your heart that you will eventually achieve your goals. Feel comforted that many others have done (and are doing) what you are doing.

▸ Take only one course at a time if you are a part-time student. It is enough responsibility with all the other things going on in your life.

▸ When you have reading assignments, try reading the last few pages of the chapter first before starting at the beginning. This will give you an idea about where the author is planning to take the argument. Often it's easier to understand where the argument is going if you know at the beginning where it's headed.

- Learn techniques for reading quickly. Read the first few paragraphs and then every second or third paragraph. Or read the first few paragraphs and then the first and last line of each paragraph.

- ▶ Try to see your education as a journey to improve your life, not necessarily just for career advancement; this will help you stay positive and not get discouraged; remember the biggest challenge is not to quit.

- ▶ Simplify your life and learn to say no.

- ▶ Do the most important family chores and tasks first. Leave the others to later.

- ▶ Put things back in the same place so that you do not forget where they are or have to waste time looking for them again.

- ▶ Be an equal opportunity employer: share the chores with your children and spouse. Let family members make their own beds and lunches. If you've enlisted their support for your goals in advance, they'll be glad to contribute.

- ▶ Clean as you go so that chores do not pile up and appear insurmountable.

- ▶ While gardening, ironing, driving the car, or doing the dishes, play your study tapes or memorize your flash cards. Make these times do double duty if the task or chore does not require much concentration.

- Plan simple meals and make use of time-savers such as microwave preparation. Eat out if it fits your budget and lifestyle; use coupons to help with the cost.

- Minimize entertaining if that's what's best for you. Hold co-operative and pot luck events if you like to entertain.

- Time yourself while doing chores. If it takes half an hour to do the dishes, try to reduce it to 15 minutes. This will make you work more efficiently. Knowing how long each task takes will also help you plan your day better.

- Temporarily store items that need cleaning or special care, such as rugs, mats, knickknacks, table cloths.

- Hire a student to do big chores for you, such as cleaning windows and blinds. If you are on a limited budget then find a student that will do cleaning in exchange for you tutoring them with their studies.

- When possible, share baby-sitting costs with other students. Hire one baby-sitter and have everyone take their children there.

- Take your family to your college or university and show them classrooms, cafeteria, library, and other interesting features of the institution. This will make them feel part of your journey.

✏️ Be creative in making sure that you have quality time with your partner or spouse. For example, your spouse could do some volunteer work while you are taking a course. After class you could meet and go out to a club or for coffee and dessert. This way you have a night out, contribute to your community and/or career, and have something new and interesting to share.

▶ Recognize up-front that you will probably be tired. It will be a 'happy' tired, however, because you'll know you are building the future you want.

▶ If you watch television, make use of commercial time to review or edit work or read your flash cards. One hour of television provides at least 10 minutes that can contribute to your overall homework and study plan.

▶ If you have a job with regular coffee and lunch breaks, do some reading during this time so that you do not have as much to do in the evening.

▶ Show your children that studying and learning are fun. For example, if you are taking a psychology course, show them some simple exercises on perception.

▶ Do homework at the same time as your children and at the same table; this will give you more quality family time and demonstrate to them the importance of applying oneself to do well at school.

- Share stories with your children about your professor and homework. This will create a more open environment for them to talk to you about their school likes and dislikes.

- If there are celebrations or theatre productions at your college or university make them family outings. Many of these productions are free or cost very little.

- Exercise, eat well, and get enough sleep. Review flash cards or listen to tapes while exercising. Exercise with children and other family members, so that work-out time becomes family time.

Always bear in mind that your own resolution to succeed is more important than any other one thing.

Abraham Lincoln

PERSONAL NOTES

How long does it take to do the chores listed below? What will be your new shorter time goal? Add other chores to the list if needed.

PRIMARY CHORES	CURRENT TIME	TIME GOAL
Laundry	_____	_____
Ironing	_____	_____
Washing dishes	_____	_____
Drying dishes	_____	_____
Loading/unloading dishwasher	_____	_____
Washing floors	_____	_____
Vacuuming	_____	_____
Grocery shopping	_____	_____
Putting away groceries	_____	_____
Making meals	_____	_____
Washing the car	_____	_____
Cutting the lawn	_____	_____
Upkeep of garden	_____	_____

How will you integrate your learning into your home and work life?

HOME	WORK

What is your educational goal for the next year?

_____

What family chores can you delegate?

_____

How can you share babysitting costs with other students?

_____

What are some cost saving measures you could adopt?

_____

What specific things can you do to enhance quality time with your children and spouse/partner?

_____

_____

How will you reward yourself for your accomplishments?

_____

_____

How will you thank others for helping you?

_____

_____

Other comments.

_____

_____

Enlisting Your Employer's Help

✎ The key to success is using flexible work policies and leave options that may be available to help you reach your goal.

▶ Many employers differentiate between courses that are directly related to your job and those that are for personal development purposes. Regardless of the category applicable to the courses you want to take, managers often have discretion about whether to approve your request for support. It therefore pays to make a strong case for support for both scenarios.

▶ Always ask for 100 per cent reimbursement for your courses and books. Let the organization decide whether it will meet this request or offer an alternative arrangement. It's not an all or nothing situation. Be prepared to negotiate. If your 100 per cent reimbursement request is refused, ask for 80 per cent, or 50, or 25.

▶ You may also have to request time off during the day to attend classes, do research, or conduct other course-related activities. There are many ways to do this: use vacation time; keep a log of your time off and 'repay' the hours through overtime or other ways of making up the time; take advantage of flexible work options if your employer offers them, such as a compressed work week for the duration of the course.

- Consider taking a leave of absence from your job. Check into the various options available at your organization. Think about taking a half-year or full year off, so that you can complete a number of courses quickly.

- Plant the idea early. Let your work colleagues and manager know that you are thinking about taking time off within the next year. It usually takes a full year for an agreement on education leave to be negotiated and approved. This also provides time for everyone to get comfortable with the idea that you are expecting to attend college or university for a year and that you will be asking for a reimbursement. Develop different options and negotiate with your manager.

- Try to involve and engage your colleagues and manager in your studies as you do your family. Let them know about your progress. Thank them for helping you. For example, write an article in your organization newspaper about the benefits of adult learning and thank your co-workers and manager in the article.

- People may try to discourage you from going to college/ university as a mature student, but remember that many people have gone later in life and have accomplished their goals. Don't let anyone or anything get in your way. Be tenacious and persevere.

Our greatest glory is not in never failing, but in rising up every time we fail.

Ralph Waldo Emerson

PERSONAL NOTES

What flexible work policies exist in your organization?

_____

What leave options are available?

_____

Who should you contact to discuss flexible work and leave options?

_____

What mature students do you know who have used policies or leave options to meet their goals?

_____

What are the obstacles to obtaining leave or flexible work arrangements?

_____

_____

How will you overcome them?

_____

What are your best options?

_____

_____

_____

What concessions are you willing to make to get your request approved?

_____

_____

How will you present these options to your manager and when? What's the benefit for the manager of supporting your training?

_____

_____

_____

When will you meet with your manager? How will you thank your manager or colleagues for supporting you in your objectives?

_____

_____

What will you do to ensure that you maintain your motivation?

_____

_____

Other Comments.

_____

_____

_____

_____

EXCELLING AT INTERVIEWS

Applying for a Job

✏️ Remember that you are embarking on an adventure. Be enthusiastic and try to see the possibilities that lie before you. Relish this journey—the challenges, the people you will meet, and the new experiences you will have.

▶ Research where you can apply for jobs, focus on the types of work you would like to do, based on your skills and education, and develop a plan to meet your career objectives. Be sure to ask for a copy of the company's organization chart and its mandate and mission. You may also want to ask for their business plan or any other information that will give you a better understanding of the organization and job.

▶ Write your résumé. Consult books showing different styles and choose one that best suits your needs and the kind of job you're looking for. It should be accurate and short; proof-read it to ensure that there are no mistakes.

- The résumé should be clean and wrinkle-free (e.g., no fingerprints, food spills).

- Send résumé in an 8 1/2" x 11" envelope so that you do not need to fold it. Put the front page on coloured paper (pastel colour) so that your résumé will stand out from the others.

- Call the office to which you are sending the résumé to verify the address and let them know that you will be sending it.

- If you fax your résumé, also send a clean original in the mail.

- Call to ensure that it was received by the organization.

- If you hand deliver the résumé, introduce yourself and tell the person why you are there. Get that person's name and number for follow-up.

- Be professionally dressed, as you may happen to meet the manager when you drop off the résumé. The manager's first impression may influence future decisions.

- If a conflict exists regarding the time of the examination or interview, ask to have your date and/or time changed. (Organizations are used to this, and it will demonstrate that you are able to assign priorities among your responsibilities and make decisions.)

- Be cheerful when you call; people will remember this.

- Remember that you never get a second chance to make a first impression.

Preparing for a Job-Related Examination

✎ Inquire about who can answer your questions about the job you are applying for, i.e., the manager or the human resource person.

▶ If you have any special needs, you should let them know right away.

▶ Ask whether the exam will be written in longhand or whether a computer will be available.

▶ Will the computer be a laptop and will it have a regular mouse?

▶ How long is the exam? If it is more than 2 hours, will there be a health break?

▶ What are the key areas to study?

▶ Are the questions weighted or not?

▶ Will we know which questions are more important than others?

▶ Are the questions multiple-choice, essay, fill-in-the-blanks, or a combination?

▶ Will the information be sent to us (English or French)?

▶ Does a pass guarantee an interview, or is there a specific passing grade?

▶ If you are not screened in, then ask for a debriefing to see where you can improve for next time.

Preparing for an interview

✏️ Where, when, and for how long?

▶ Ask how many people will be interviewing you and what their role is in terms of the position you are applying for.

▶ Determine choice of language for interview.

▶ Be prepared for general questions:
- why do you want this job?
- what skills/education do you bring to this position?
- what do you know about this organization/product/ type of work, etc.?
- why should we choose you?
- what are your strengths and/or weaknesses?
- do you have other job prospects? (You are not obligated to answer this question. Remember you are competing for a job, so do not give away information that could jeopardize your chances. You may have other job prospects, but unless you have accepted another job offer, you are still not employed. It's better just to say that you are leaving all your options open.)

▶ Have fun by role playing with a friend or relative before the interview so that your answers flow freely during the interview. Practise introductions and exits. Practise answering some of your questions in front of the mirror, so that you learn how to speak clearly and at a medium pace. This will build your confidence.

- ▶ Dressing for an interview:
  - hair is clean and groomed
  - hands and nails are clean and manicured (no chipped nail polish or outlandish colours)
  - don't wear perfume or cologne and don't smell of smoke or garlic.
  - no gum or candy
  - have clean and pressed clothes (no T-shirts, jeans, halter-tops, or see-through blouses)
  - have clean shoes, usually no running shoes

- ▶ The interview process can be very stimulating and rewarding—enjoy the ride.

During the Interview

- ✏ Think of this as a positive situation.

- ▶ Be confident. Relax and smile—if you're having difficulty doing this, pretend you are acting for a part in a play.

- ▶ Do not chew gum or candy unless you have a bad cold and need a lozenge.

- ▶ Stay focused, look interested and do not fidget.

- ▶ Take time to think; remember you want to give a good answer.

- ▶ Bring a pad and pencil. Bring a small bottle of water if you think you may want a drink.

- ▶ If you have to write down the question and then some points before speaking, this is acceptable (the interviewer will wait).

- ▶ Sit and stand tall with your head up.

- ▶ Speak in an enthusiastic way, not in a monotone. Also, do not speak too quickly.

- ▶ Make eye contact with everyone in the room (you may have more than one interviewer).

Post Examination/Interview

- ✏️ Call and ask to meet with the interviewer or ask if you can have a debriefing over the telephone.

- ▶ When you meet, ask for the strengths and weaknesses of your interview performance.

- ▶ Remain objective and professional while hearing where you can improve.

- ▶ Write down what the interviewer says so you can work on areas where you need to improve.

- ▶ File notes at home to review before the next interview.

- ▶ Thank the interviewer at the end of meeting for taking the time to meet with you.

- ▶ Send a brief letter or card the next day saying thank you (this is both a courtesy and a networking technique).

▶ Reward yourself for your hard work.

Points to Remember

✐ The interview process is much more than just a competition for one job. The interviewer may have other positions in other areas. Interviews are often for more than one job, even if they do not tell you.

▶ Contact the organization every year (put it on your calendar now) whether you are working or not (send a letter and résumé and follow up with a call) as part of your ongoing networking strategy. You never know when you may want to work for this organization or when they may have an opening. Also, they may have colleagues or friends who are hiring.

▶ The night before the exam or interview eat properly and get plenty of sleep.

▶ Always leave on a positive note; shake hands as you depart.

▶ Getting a job is hard work—never let your guard down—persevere, and be relentless in your approach.

▶ You never know who will be the 'link to your success', so make the most out of each interview.

▶ Even if you are not the successful candidate, this does not necessarily mean that you didn't do well. It just means that you weren't the right 'fit' for a particular position. Therefore, be proud and congratulate yourself for making it through the examination and/or interview stage.

Make the most of
yourself, for that is
all there is of you.

Ralph Waldo Emerson

What types of résumés exist and which is best suited to the job you are applying for?

_____

_____

_____

_____

Where would you like to apply for a job?

_____

_____

_____

What types of work would you like to do?

_____

_____

_____

What skills do you have?

_____

_____

_____

What education do you have?

_____

_____

_____

What are your career objectives?

_____

_____

_____

How and when will you achieve them?

_____

_____

_____

What information should you get about the organization and job?

_____

_____

_____

Who can help you prepare (including role playing) for the interview?

_____

_____

_____

_____

What will you write in your thank-you note to the interviewer?
Make the note sincere and short.

_____

_____

_____

In your post-interview or conversation, what were considered your
strengths? Where do you need to make improvements?

_____

_____

_____

How will you further develop your strengths?

_____

_____

_____

How will you make improvements?

_____

_____

_____

_____

_____

How will you reward yourself for going through each step of the interview process?

_____

_____

_____

Other comments.

_____

_____

_____

_____

_____

_____

_____

ORDER FORM

If you would like additional copies please send the following information, accompanied with a money order or certified cheque (no C.O.D.) to this address: **KNG Enterprises**
P.O. Box 71007
L'Esplanade Laurier
181 Bank Street
Ottawa, Ontario, Canada
K2P 2L9

_____

NAME

_____

ADDRESS

_____

CITY

_____

PROVINCE/STATE

_____

COUNTRY

_____

POSTAL/ZIP CODE

Method of Payment: Certified cheque: ___   Money Order: ___
Inside Canada, $15.95 (Cdn) plus $3.00 (Cdn) for shipping and handlng.
Outside Canada, $11.95 (US) plus $3.00 (US) for shipping and handling.

Total Order: _____ Book(s) **x** $ _____ **=** $ _____

(+ shipping)   _____

(= sub-total)   _____

(+ GST or HST for Canada)   _____

(Total Amount Due)   _____

Allow 6 to 8 weeks delivery. Thank you for your interest in this book and we wish you every success with your studies.